TREE of LIFE

INCARNATION, PASSION & GLORY

Saint Bonaventure on the Christ Story

edited by
Stephen Joseph Wolf

idjc press

D1707557

Tree of Life
Incarnation, Passion & Glory
Saint Bonaventure on the Christ Story
Copyright © 2012
Stephen Joseph Wolf

Songs are in the public domain and
previously appeared in *Hinge Hour Singer*.

Ink and brush images are by Stephen Joseph Wolf.

printed and distributed by Ingram
published by idjc press
www.idjc.org

ISBN 978-1-937081-05-8

E Book edition ISBN 978-1-937081-15-7

TREE OF LIFE

MYSTERY OF THE INCARNATION   WEEK ONE

1st Fruit: His Distinguished Origin   9
    Begotten of God   10
    Prefigured   11
    Sent from Heaven   13
    Born of Mary   15
2nd Fruit: The Humility of his Way of Life
    Conformed to his Ancestors   16
    Shown to the Magi   17
    Submissive to the Law   18
    Exiled from his Kingdom   19

    WEEK TWO

3rd Fruit: The Loft of his Power   23
    Heavenly Baptist   24
    Tempted by the Enemy   25
    Wonderful in his Miracles   26
    Transfigured   27
4th Fruit: The Plenitude of his Piety
    The Solicitous Shepherd   29
    Bathed with Tears   30
    Acclaimed King of the World   31
    Consecrated Bread   32

MYSTERY OF HIS PASSION   WEEK THREE

5th Fruit: His Confidence in Trials   35
    Sold through Guile   36
    Prostrate in Prayer   37
    Surrounded by the Mob   39
    Bound with Chains   40
6th Fruit: His Patience in Bad Treatment
    Denied by his Own   41
    Blindfolded   42
    Handed Over to Pilate   43
    Condemned to Death   44

WEEK FOUR

7th Fruit: His Constancy Under Torture   47
        Scorned by All   48
        Nailed to the Cross   49
        Linked with Thieves   50
        Given Gall to Drink   51
8th Fruit: Victory in the Conflict of Death
        Sun Dimmed in Death   52
        Pierced with a Lance   53
        Dressed in Blood   55
        Laid in the Tomb   56

MYSTERY OF HIS GLORY   WEEK FIVE

9th Fruit: The Novelty of his Resurrection   59
        Triumphant in Death   60
        Rising in Blessedness   61
        Extraordinary Beauty   63
        Dominion over the Earth   65
10th Fruit: The Sublimity of his Ascension
        Leader of his Army   66
        Lifted Up to Heaven   67
        Giver of the Spirit   69
        Freeing from Guilt   71
                                  WEEK SIX
11th Fruit: The Equity of his Judgment   75
        Truthful Witness   77
        Wrathful Judge   78
        Glorious Conqueror   79
        Adorned Spouse   80
12th Fruit: The Eternity of his Kingdom
        King and Son of the King   81
        Inscribed Book   83
        Fountain-Ray of Light   84
        Desired End   86

        Prayer to the Holy Spirit   89

Sources   92

How to Use *Tree of Life*

These fifty meditation renderings have two kinds of users in mind.

1st - an Individual Seeker

reflecting on the mystery and person of Jesus Christ:

> Take the time to go slowly, and keep it simple.
>
> Wherever you find yourself drawn, linger for pondering, perhaps breathing with a particular word or phrase.
>
> Consider one meditation each day for fifty days:
> > Treat page 7 as the first meditation and
> > ignore the six "weekly" beginnings.
> > Begin anytime or appropriately on:
> > > December 21 (puts the Nativity on December 25),
> > > or the Second Sunday of Lent
> > > > (puts Easter on Easter Sunday),
> > > or August 16 (puts the Crucifixion on September 14)

2nd – a Faith Sharing Group

meeting over six weeks:

> Use what is helpful and ignore the rest; keep it simple.
>
> If someone in the group knows the song, you have a song leader. If one person leads the rest can follow, because the tunes are simple and from the Church tradition.
>
> Group members can take turns being the *Leader* week to week, but it works best if there is only one *Leader* of each session.
>
> Within each session, group members can take turns being the *Reader,* though no one should be compelled to be a *Reader.*
>
> The *Leader* is encouraged to allow, by timing it, one full minute of silence before announcing the next meditation.

But keep it simple.

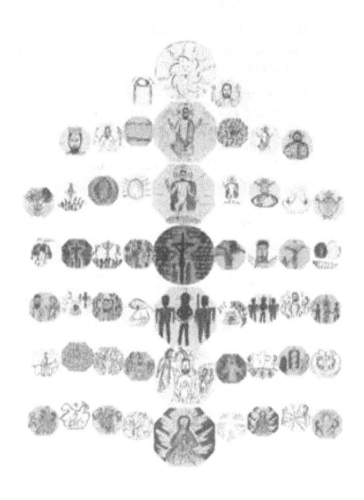

OPENING MEDITATION

Leader: **Imagine a tree.**

Reader:

Its roots draw water from a perpetual fountain that becomes a great river alive with four streams giving water to the whole Church. From the trunk of this tree see the twelve branches, each full of leaves and flowers and fruit. The leaves are the medicine that prevents and heals every kind of sickness. The flowers radiate each beautiful color and every perfume aroma, waking up worried hearts, attracting human desire. The twelve fruits, with every delight and pleasing taste, offered for servants of God to eat and be satisfied to always with their taste, are one undivided fruit with a variety of consolations. This fruit of the Virgin womb reaches its savory maturity on the tree of the cross under the mid-day heat of the Eternal Sun that is the love of Christ.

one full minute of silence, then:

Leader: Please turn to page (   ) for Week (   ).

The an-gel Ga-bri-el from heav-en came,
With wings as drift-ed snow and eyes as flame;
"All hail," the an-gel said, "O low-ly place,
Most high-ly fa-vored maid-en, full of grace."
Of her would come the Christ Em-man-u-el;
With all the an-gels, "Glo-ri-a!" we tell.

"For know a bless-ed Moth-er you shall be,
All gen-er-a-tions' praise e-ter-nal-ly;
Your Son shall be Em-man-u-el, fore-told,
Most high-ly fa-vored la-dy, from of old."
Of her would come the Christ Em-man-u-el;
With all the an-gels, "Glo-ri-a!" we tell.

Then gen-tle Ma-ry meek-ly bowed her head;
"To me be as it pleas-es God!" she said.
"My soul shall laud and mag-ni-fy the Name."
Most high-ly fa-vored la-dy, liv-ing flame.
Of her would come the Christ Em-man-u-el;
With all the an-gels, "Glo-ri-a!" we tell.

Text: from *Birjina gaztettobat zegoen,* traditional Basque Carol; translated by
Sabine Baring-Gould, d.1924, altered significantly for a different melody
Music: 10 10 10 10 10 10 UNDE ET MEMORES, William H. Monk, d.1899
Popular melody for: *Lord Who At The First Eucharist Did Pray*

WEEK ONE

1st Fruit: His Distinguished Origin
Begotten of God, Prefigured,
Sent from Heaven, Born of Mary
2nd Fruit: The Humility of his Way of Life
Conformed to his Ancestors, Shown to the Magi,
Submissive to the Law, Exiled from his Kingdom

Opening Meditation from page 7.

Song from page 8.

Leader: God has a plan.
Each of us is a part of that plan.

Just in case
no one has ever said this to you,
God loves you.

Sooner or later, each of us will be called
to deal with the truth
of God's complete love of you and me.

If not yet, why not now?

Our process is simple. We will take turns reading one paragraph at a time. If reading in public is not your thing, just say "pass, please." We will spend one full minute of silence after each meditation.

Leader: **Begotten of God**

Reader:

With eyes of a dove or an eagle, gaze on what you see: that Eternal Light, so simple as to be unmeasureable, so brilliant as to seem hidden, from which emerges a splendor, coeternal and coequal and consubstantial, the power and wisdom of the Father. In him the Father gives from eternity order to all things, created and governed and guided to the glory of God, by nature and grace and justice and mercy, so that nothing is left without its place in the world.

one full minute of silence after each meditation

Prefigured

In the creation beginning a nature paradise is given the parents of humanity, who after the eating from the tree forbidden are driven out. Since that day unceasing mercy calls straying humans to a good penance way by (*a*) hope of being forgiven and (*b*) the promise of a Savior. Knowing our ungrateful ignorance, the Son's coming is announced and promised and prefigured by God through the five ages of patriarchs and matriarchs, judges, priests, kings, and prophets, from Abel the Just to John the Baptist. Human minds are stirred to faith and human hearts inflame with living desire.

Sent from Heaven

The fullness of time has come. As on the sixth day the *'adam* was formed from earth in the divine hand, so the sixth age begins with the sending of arch-messenger Gabriel to the Virgin, who says her "yes!" Upon her comes divine fire, her soul inflamed, her flesh made holy, shadowed in protection by the power of the Most High. And so comes the Person of the Son, human and divine, not created but of both God and Mary begotten-generated, the same Person God and human, the properties of each maintaining. You too would sing that hymn,

My soul is stretched and stretches full
with the glory of God!

Born of Mary

The reign of Caesar Augustus, a quiet silence of universal peace, makes possible a census of the world. So divine providence guides the husband Joseph with the pregnant young girl of royal descent to Bethlehem, the *house of bread.* Nine months having passed, the King of Peace comes forth from the virgin womb like a bridegroom from his bridal chamber. Great and rich, for us he becomes small and poor, born in an unfamiliar stable, wrapped in swaddling clothes, nourished by virginal milk, to lie in a feeding box between an ox and an ass. Let your soul embrace the divine manger, press your lips to kiss the boy's feet, and sing

Glory to God in the highest!
And on earth peace
to people of good will.

Conformed to his Ancestors

It is the tradition: On the eighth day the boy is circumcised and named Jesus (*God saves*). Without delay he shows himself the true Savior promised by word and sign, one like us in all things but ignorance and sin, in humility, the guard and root of all virtues.

What, dust and ash, is your reason for pride?
Why flee from the remedy of eternal salvation?
Be willing to follow the humble Savior.

Shown to the Magi

In Judah the Bethlehem birth, while far off in the east a star shows to the Magi the way to the home of the humble King.

Join the company of the holy kings,
accept the testimony of the Hebrew Scriptures,
venerate Christ the King
with gold and incense and myrrh,
avert the evil of the fearing king,
return to your own country,
and be your part
of the first fruits of the Gentiles.

Submissive to the Law

The teacher of perfect humility, equal to the
Father in all things, submits himself to the Law
in the humility of the most pure Virgin who
nevertheless observes the law of purification.
The redeemer of all sons and daughters is
redeemed as a firstborn son and presented to
God in the temple in the presence of the just.
Rejoice with blessed old Simeon and aged
Anna. Be not bashful. Have no fear. Take your
turn with aged Anna, the Infant in your arms.
Dance with blessed old Simeon and sing his
song:

Now dismiss your free-slave, Lord,
according to your word in peace.

Exiled from his Kingdom

Humility is dressed in the company of poverty knowing better than riches, patience in bearing insults with dignity, and obedience in following the bidding of others. By God's protective design the tiny King is taken to Egypt as a pilgrim and pauper. Killed, as it were, in the slaughter of children his own age, these instead of him, and after the death of the mind-sick "great" king, brought back to Judah for growing in wisdom-age-grace, subject to parents, but true to the nature of a twelve-year-old, allows the sorrow of the searching mother of so tender and handsome a boy.

Pondering Week One

His Distinguished Origin & The Humility of his Way of Life

Ponder in silence whether in these meditations
something like one of these surfaced:

a seed planted,

> something I anticipate taking root and
> growing within me, and growing me…

a memory provoked,

> part of my story or our journey,
> whether pleasant or sad…

a question raised,

> something unknown
> to study, research, discuss with others,
> or further ponder…

an action prompted

> or a way to let God grow me into the
> human person God created me to be…

*Allow at least three minutes for silent pondering,
and then the group may either discuss the ponderings
(restraining the urge to "fix" anybody)
or stay in silence until time is up.*

When time is up: Are there any intercessions
from the group?

Our Father ...   *and a stanza from
the song on page 8?*

All glo-ry, laud, and hon-or,
> to you, re-deem-er, King,
To whom the lips of chil-dren
> make sweet ho-san-nas ring.
The King you are of Is-ra-el,
> and Da-vid's roy-al Son,
Be-lov-ed of the Fa\-ther,
> our Roy-al Bless-ed One.

The com-pa-ny of an-gels
> are prais-ing you on high,
With hu-man be-ings too all
> cre-a-tion makes re-ply.
The Cho-sen of the Cov-e-nant
> with psalms be-fore you went;
So too our praise and an\-thems
> be-fore you we pre-sent.

To you, be-fore your pass-ion,
> A-pos-tles sang your praise;
To you, now high ex-al-ted,
> our mel-o-dy we raise.
Ac-cep-ta-ble their voi\-ces;
> hear too the praise we bring:
De-light in your be-lov\-ed,
> our Sa-vior and our King.

Text: St. Theodulph of Orleans, 821?, for Palm Sunday;
translated by John M. Neal, 1854, altered
Music: 76 76 D, ST. THEODULPH, Melchior Teschner, 1613

WEEK TWO

3rd Fruit: The Loft of his Power
> Heavenly Baptist, Tempted by the Enemy,
> Wonderful in his Miracles, Transfigured

4th Fruit: The Plenitude of his Piety
> The Solicitous Shepherd, Bathed with Tears,
> Acclaimed King of the World, Consecrated Bread

Opening Meditation from page 7.

Song from page 22.

Leader: Jesus, the Son of God, has a plan.
Each of us is a part of that plan.

Just in case no one has ever said this to
you, your vocation is part of his mission.

Sooner or later, each Christian will be
called to decide whether to accept the
way of Christ as his or her own way.

If not yet, if not now, when?

Our process is simple. We will take turns
reading one paragraph at a time. If reading in
public is not your thing, just say "pass, please."
We will spend one full minute of silence after
each meditation.

Leader: **Heavenly Baptist**

Reader:

At thirty years of age the Savior begins his saving work, choosing to act before teaching, baptism being the sacrament doorway and the virtue foundation. His desire to be baptized by John shows forth the model of perfection justice and confers the regenerative power onto water by contact with his flesh.

Be in his company, regenerated in his mystery.
Explore the Jordan shore
and hear the Father in the voice,
and see the Son in the flesh
and the Holy Spirit in the dove.
Let the heaven of the Trinity open up to you.

reminder: one full minute of silence after each meditation

Tempted by the Enemy

Jesus is led by the Spirit into the desert to be
tempted by the evil one. Humility endures the
enemy attack making us humble, in a victory
win giving us courage, in a hard and solitary
way arousing faithful souls to strive in strength
to endure hardships.

Come, disciple-student of Christ;
seek with your Teacher the solitude secrets.
Companion of wild beasts, share his silence
and daylong fasting and three encounters
with the clever tempter. Learn your recourse
in every temptation crisis to the one tested
as are we, like us in all things but sin.

Wonderful in his Miracles

Things of marvel: elements changed, loaves multiplied, a sea walked upon, waves calmed, demons silenced, sick cured, lepers cleansed, and dead raised; blind see, deaf hear, mute speak, crippled walk, paralytics move, and withered limbs are given senses.

Our conscience calls with the leper:
Lord, if you wish, you can make me clean.
Now with the centurion: *Lord, my servant boy is lying at home paralyzed and is suffering intently.*
Now with the woman of Canaan:
Son of David, have mercy on me.
Now with the bleeding woman:
If I touch his garment, I will be cured.
And now with Mary and Martha:
See, Lord, the one you love is ill.

Transfigured

The strength of hope is given to the human spirit in Peter, James and John, taken by Jesus up a high mountain, just them. Word reveals the Trinity mystery. Word foretells the Passion rejection. Word shows the coming Resurrection Glory in the Transfiguration of Now. Both Law and Prophecy give testimony to him in the sight of Moses and Elijah and the voice and cloud of the Father and Holy Spirit.

You soul, devoted to Christ, say with Peter,
Lord, it is good for us to be here.

The Solicitous Shepherd

How great is the mercy of the Good Shepherd in devoted affection for the hundredth lost sheep, sought with care, found with joy, and brought home on his very shoulders. *The good shepherd gives his life for his sheep.* He means to fulfill the prophecy: *Like a shepherd he will feed his flock* and so endures toil, anxiety and lack of food, travels to towns and villages, preaches the kingdom of God, and through dangers and plottings passes nights in watchful prayer. Fearless before critics, affable to inquirers, affectionate to the repentant, he calls his own variety of Matthew, Zaccheus, the sinful woman at his feet, and one accused of adultery.

With Matthew, follow him.
With Zaccheus, receive him with hospitality.
Join the sinful woman and anoint his feet and
wash them with your own tears and hair.
Hear in your own ears the mercy words heard:
Nor do I condemn you;
go and sin no more.

Bathed with Tears

The fountain of mercy, the good Jesus, weeps for us many times: over Lazarus, over Jerusalem, and on the cross a flood of tears to wipe out all sins. Abundance weeps the Savior, now over the misery of human weakness, now over the night of a blind heart, now over the depravity of stubborn malice.

When hard is your heart, insane to be impious,
why rejoice and laugh like a madman
while Wisdom herself weeps over you?
Be not bereft of true life,
but consider your physician
who weeps to make you well.

Acclaimed King of the World

Lazarus is raised and ointment is poured over the head of Jesus. The fragrance of his fame has spread and he mounts an ass, humility model in the people's palm branch applause and garments thrown on the way. Compassion is praised in a city to be destroyed, a lament.

Rise now, you servant of your Savior,
gather your piety and virtue,
your olive branches and palms,
and follow now
the Lord of heaven and earth,
sitting on the back of an ass.

Consecrated Bread

Remember the last banquet, the sacred supper: both paschal lamb and Immaculate Lamb are given as food. He dines at the one same table and our humble King of Glory washes the feet of fisher and betrayer. Soon to be the sacrifice pleasing to God, the priceless redemption price, our viaticum and our sustenance, he gives his sacred body and true blood as food and drink. He gives Peter another warning and offers John the resting place of his breast.

> *As a deer longs for springs of water,*
> *so my soul longs for you, O God.*

Pondering Week Two

The Loft of his Power & The Plenitude of his Piety

Ponder in silence whether in these meditations
something like one of these surfaced:

a seed planted,
> something I anticipate taking root and
> growing within me, and growing me…

a memory provoked,
> part of my story or our journey,
> whether pleasant or sad…

a question raised,
> something unknown
> to study, research, discuss with others,
> or further ponder…

an action prompted
> or a way to say "yes" to the call to be the
> human person God created me to be…

*Allow at least three minutes for silent pondering,
and then the group may either discuss the ponderings
(restraining the urge to "fix" anybody)
or stay in silence until time is up.*

When time is up: Are there any intercessions
from the group?

Our Father … *and a stanza from the song on page 22?*

Je-sus, my Lord\, **my God**/, **my all**\;
How late, my Je-sus, have I sought.
You pour down rich\-es of/ your grace\;
How can I love you as I ought?
Je-sus, our Lord, we you a-dore!
Call us to love you more/ and more\.
Call us to love you more and more.

Je-sus, what could you have found/ in me\?
How great the joy that you have brought!
How have you dealt\ so pa/-tient-ly\?
So far ex-ceed-ing hope or thought!
Je-sus, our Lord, we you a-dore!
Call us to love you more/ and more\.
Call us to love you more and more.

Had I but Ma\-ry's sin/-less heart\
With which to love you, dear-est King;
O! with what bursts\ of fer/-vent praise\
Your good-ness, Je-sus, would I sing.
Sweet Sac-ra-ment, we you a-dore!
Call us to love you more/ and more\.
Call us to love you more and more.

Text: Henry A. Collins, 1854, altered;
vs. 3 Frederick W. Faber, d. 1863, altered
Music: SWEET SACRAMENT, LM with refrain,
Romischkatholisches Gesanguchlein , 1826

WEEK THREE

5th Fruit: His Confidence in Trials
Sold through Guile, Prostrate in Prayer,
Surrounded by the Mob, Bound with Chains

6th Fruit: His Patience in Bad Treatment
Denied by his Own, Blindfolded,
Handed Over to Pilate, Condemned to Death

Opening Meditation from page 7.

Song from page 34.

Leader: God has a plan.
Each of us is a part of that plan.

Just in case no one has ever told you,
God's truth is complete love for you.

Sooner or later, each of us will be called
to speak a prophetic truth God will want
a person or a group of people to hear,
perhaps even at risk of a real cost.

When might I expect to be ready for this?

Our process is simple. We will take turns
reading one paragraph at a time. If reading in
public is not your thing, just say "pass, please."
We will spend one full minute of silence after
each meditation.

Leader: **Sold through Guile**

Reader:

The traitor is filled with the poison of deceit, aflame with greed to seek a cheap reward, ungrateful for his apostolic dignity, and hardened even to banquet intimacy.

The meek Lamb of God
can help those left at wits end by companions
and even best friends who let them down.
You cannot demand another to be like Jesus,
but you can ask for yourself the grace to do
what he in whom no guile was to be found did,
the grace to give even a betrayer the chance
to let his or her heart be softened.

reminder: one full minute of silence after each meditation

Prostrate in Prayer

Knowing what is to happen to him, Jesus sings hallel psalms, and goes to the Mount of Olives to pray with his Father, as is his custom. The Shepherd's sheep are about to be dispersed and the death imagining is a horror to his senses: *Father if it be possible,*
let this cup pass from me.
Intense anxiety springs from the Redeemer in bloody drops of sweat gathering to the ground.

Lord Jesus, Ruler,
your exhibition of human nature
tells the truth that you carry our sorrows
and that your passion is of real pain.

Surrounded by the Mob

When men of blood come at night with the betrayer and torches and lanterns and weapons, Jesus readily hurries to offer himself plainly to them. For our assurance that world power can do nothing against him unless he permit it, the guards are thrown to the ground. But the kind touch of his hand heals the ear of the opposition servant cut off by his own disciple. He restrains the violent zeal of human defense.

Bound with Chains

Hear how they lay hands on the King of Glory
to bind his innocent hands in chains same as a
thief, dragging as to a sacrifice with insult but
without objection. A grief stings and penetrates
the disciples' hearts, and driven by remorse the
Judas is so bitter as to prefer to die than to live.
He despairs when he could have returned to
the fountain of mercy. O the grief.

Denied by his Own

The Master is captured and the disciples flee. More faithful, Peter follows at a distance. At a maid's query, he denies knowing Christ, and by oath and three times. The cock crows and the kind Master looks upon his beloved disciple with mercy and grace. Peter weeps in bitter tears.

Whoever you are, remember the passion of your beloved Master; go with Peter to Jesus and when they look upon you, accept with Peter the bitter two-fold inebriation: remorse for yourself and compassion for Christ and be filled with the spirit of holiness.

Blindfolded

Our High Priest Jesus Christ confesses to the
high priests his true identity: the Son of God.
As if it were blasphemy, he is condemned to
die, given to insults, defiled by spit, beaten by
human hands, struck on the ears, and derided.

True and kind Jesus,
what soul devoted to you can see and hear this
and restrain from tears
or hide the sorrow of inner compassion?

Handed Over to Pilate

Raging as mad wild beasts, they expose the life of the Just One to a judge thought of as a mad dog! The high priests demand death by torture on the cross and he stands before his judge in silent patience.

Just Jesus, who will be so hardened
as not to groan and cry out in spirit when
hearing or pondering those horrible shouts?:
We have no king but Caesar!
Away with him! Away with him! Crucify him!

Condemned to Death

Pilate knows envy when he sees it, and finds
clearly no cause at all for killing. After Herod
returns Jesus, he is stripped for public mockery
and savage scourging, bruise upon bruise and
wound upon wound.

And you, lost human
and cause of all this confusion and sorrow,
how do you not break down and weep?
Join the crowd and behold the innocent Lamb
condemned to an unjust sentence to rescue you
and pay back for you what he did not steal.

Pondering Week Three
His Confidence in Trials & His Patience in Bad Treatment

Ponder in silence whether in these meditations something like one of these surfaced:

a seed planted,
> something I anticipate taking root and growing within me, and growing me…

a memory provoked,
> part of my story or our journey, whether pleasant or sad…

a question raised,
> something unknown
> to study, research, discuss with others, or further ponder…

an action prompted
> or way to invite grace to overwhelm me with fearless trust in God's mercy...

Allow at least three minutes for silent pondering,
and then the group may either discuss the ponderings
(restraining the urge to "fix" anybody)
or stay in silence until time is up.

When time is up: Are there any intercessions from the group?

Our Father ... *and a stanza from the song on page 34?*

At the name of Je/-sus, ev-'ry knee shall bow,
Ev-'ry tongue con-fess/ him King of glo-ry now;
'Tis the Fa/-ther's plea\-sure that we call him Lord
Who from the be-gin\-ning is the migh-ty Word.

At his voice cre-a/-tion sprang at once to sight,
All the an-gels' fa/-ces, all the hosts of light,
Thrones and dom/-in-a\-tions,

                              stars up-on their way,
All the heav'n-ly or\-ders, in their great ar-ray.

Hum-bled for a sea/-son, to re-ceive a name
From the lips of sin/-ners un-to whom he came,
Faith-ful-ly/ he bore\ it, spot-less to the last,
Carr-ied it vic-tor\-ious

                    when from death he passed.

Bro-thers, Sis-ters, name/ him,

                    with love strong as death
But with awe and won/-der,

                    and with ba-ted breath!
He is God/ our Sa\-vior,

                    he is Christ the Lord,
Ev-er to be wor\-shipped,

                    trust-ed and a-dored.

see Philippians 2:6-11
Text: Caroline M. Noel, *The Name of Jesus and Other Verses
for the Sick and Lonely*, 1870, altered
Music: 11 11 11 11 ADORO TE DEVOTE,
Benedictine Plainsong, Mode V, 13th Century

WEEK FOUR

7th Fruit: His Constancy Under Torture
> Scorned by All, Nailed to the Cross,
> Linked with Thieves, Given Gall to Drink

8th Fruit: Victory in the Conflict of Death
> Sun Dimmed in Death, Pierced with a Lance,
> Dressed in Blood, Laid in the Tomb

Opening Meditation from page 7.

Song from page 46.

Leader: God has a plan and each of us has a part in that plan even though there be times this is difficult to see.

In case no one has ever told you, remember again: God loves you.

Sooner or later, each of us will be called to the Christian task of naming our cross, picking it up daily, and following Jesus.

If not yet, when may I be ready?

Our process is simple. We will take turns reading one paragraph at a time. If reading in public is not your thing, just say "pass, please." We will spend one full minute of silence after each meditation.

Leader: **Scorned by All**

Reader:

Pilate has given satisfaction to bad desires. Now sacrilegious fear seeks to heap a full load of mockery. In front of all in the praetorium, stripped of his clothes and dressed up in a purple cloak over a red tunic, they put a thorn-crown on his head and a reed in his hand and genuflect a mockery of hits and spits.

Take a good look, human pride
hungry for honors and running from reproach,
and be confused.
This is your King and your God
wanting to snatch you from eternal confusion
and heal you of the pride disease.

reminder: one full minute of silence after each meditation

Nailed to the Cross

Done with the insults they put his own clothes back on, and our King carries his own cross to the place of Calvary. Stripped now completely, thrown on the rough wood, spread out, pulled and stretched like an animal hide, fixed to the cross by pointed nails, wounds now tear in his hands and feet. His clothing is divided up as plunder except the raffled seamless garment.

See, my soul, our blessed God
deep in the waters of suffering:
crowned with thorns,
back bent under the cross,
stripped like a leper,
cuts and bruises on his back and sides,
fixed with nails, wound upon wound.
Might this reasonably be my longing:
to be fixed with my beloved
to the yoke of the cross?

Linked with Thieves

Outside the city the innocent Lamb is lifted on
the cross to be a spectacle among thieves, just
one more criminal for whom friends weep and
enemies scoff and passersby headshake. One
thief confesses and honors the gift of mercy.

O soul in hope of pardon,
however great a sinner you be,
hear his words: *Father, forgive them!*
and his promise: *You will be with me in paradise!*
and shrink not from following in the way
of the Lord God suffering for you.

Given Gall to Drink

Knowing it to be so, Jesus says, *I thirst,* and then, *It is finished,* bitter passion reaching complete fullness in the taste of gall and vinegar. As by the sweet taste of the fruit forbidden our ancestor Adam was brought to our perdition, how fitting that the remedy be in the contra saving direction.

Blessed Virgin,
what tongue can tell or intellect grasp
the heavy weight of your desolation?
You present at all these happenings to
this most holy flesh you chastely conceived,
nourished and held on your lap,
kissed with your lips and gazed on in love,
see now with the eye of your mind his spirit
groaning in wearied agony, anxious confusion,
and sadness; hear now his compassion for you:
Woman, behold your son.

Sun Dimmed in Death

The innocent Lamb and true Sun of Justice being three hours on the cross, in compassion for its Maker the sun hides its light for the dying outcry of Jesus, divine and human, commending his spirit into the hands of his Father. The temple veil is torn, the earth quakes, and tombs are opened. The centurion admits this man as truly God.

Lord, holy Father, look upon your Anointed.
Redeemed human, consider who he is,
how great, what kind of person
who for you hangs on the cross,
at whose death heaven and earth mourn
and hard rock cracks as if in compassion.
Human heart, are you harder still than rock?

Pierced with a Lance

The divine plan permits a soldier to pierce open his body's side with a lance. The Church is formed out of the side of Christ asleep on the cross. Blood mixes with water and flows, our salvation pouring forth in sacraments to confer the life of grace, the fountain of living water springing up to eternal life.

Beloved of Christ,
be like the dove and make your nest here
and like the sparrow finding a home
draw the saving water from this fountain,
this river, to make fertile the whole of earth.

Dressed in Blood

Christ the Lord is stained with his bleeding sweat, lashes and thorns, nails and lance. His priestly robe is red, like that of the wine presser or that of Joseph sold as a slave in the envy of his own brothers.

See again, Father of mercy,
the beast-bloody tunic of your beloved Joseph
in the body of your innocent willing Son.

See too, Mother of mercy,
the stained garment of your beloved Son
woven as true art from your chaste body,
and with the Holy Spirit beg forgiveness
for us who take refuge in you.

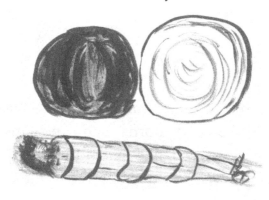

Laid in the Tomb

Another Joseph, of Arimathea, permitted by Pilate and assisted by Nicodemus, takes down the body of Jesus, wraps it in a cloth, and buries it with all reverence in the tomb meant for himself. Soldier-guards are assigned and the holy women buy spices for anointing. The disciples having fled, Mary Magdalene in the wound of impatient love bathes the tomb with her tears.

Good Jesus, my God,
grant to me, unworthy, weak of merit,
and not present at these history events,
that I may ponder them in my mind
and know toward you, my God crucified,
the feeling of compassion shared
by your innocent mother and the Magdalene
at the very hour of your passion.

Pondering Week Four

His Constancy Under Torture & Victory in the Conflict of Death

Ponder in silence whether in these meditations
something like one of these surfaced:

a seed planted,

something I anticipate taking root and
growing within me, and growing me…

a memory provoked,

part of my story or our journey,
whether pleasant or sad…

a question raised,

something unknown
to study, research, discuss with others,
or further ponder…

an action prompted

or a way that the Lord is calling me
to let go of what is not really me…

*Allow at least three minutes for silent pondering,
and then the group may either discuss the ponderings
(restraining the urge to "fix" anybody)
or stay in silence until time is up.*

When time is up: Are there any intercessions
from the group?

Our Father … *and a stanza from the song on page 46?*

Ye sons and daugh\-**ters** of\ the King,
With heav'n-ly hosts\ in glo\-ry sing,
To-day the grave\ has lost\ its sting:
                                        Al-le-lu-ia!

On that first morn\-ing of\ the week,
Be-fore the day\ be-gan\ to break,
The Ma-rys went\ their Lord\ to seek:
                                        Al-le-lu-ia!

An an-gel bade\ their sor\-row flee,
By speak-ing thus\ un-to\ the three:
"Your Lord is gone\ to Gal\-i-lee:" Al-le-lu-ia!

That night th'A-pos\-tles met\ in fear,
A-midst them came\ their Lord\ most dear
And said, "Peace be\ un-to\ you here:"
                                        Al-le-lu-ia!

Bless-ed are they\ that have\ not seen
And yet whose faith\ has con\-stant been,
In life e-ter\-nal they\ shall reign: Al-le-lu-ia!

And we with ho\-ly Church\ u-nite,
As ev-er-more\ is just\ and right,
In glo-ry to\ the King\ of light: Al-le-lu-ia!

Al-le-lu-ia\!   Al-le\-lu-ia!   Al-le-lu-ia!

Text: see John 20; attributed to Jean Tisserand, d. 1494;
translated by John M. Neal, 1851, altered
Music: 888, O FILII ET FILIAE; Chant Mode II,
Airs sur les hymnes sacrez, odes et noels, 1623

WEEK FIVE

9th Fruit: The Novelty of his Resurrection
Triumphant in Death, Rising in Blessedness,
Extraordinary Beauty, Dominion over the Earth
10th Fruit: The Sublimity of his Ascension
Leader of his Army, Lifted Up to Heaven,
Giver of the Spirit, Freeing from Guilt

Opening Meditation from page 7.

Song from page 58.

Leader: God has a plan.
Each of us is a part of that plan.

Just in case no one has ever
said this to you, God loves you.

Sooner or later, each of us will be called
to let the Christ show us his wholly new
resurrection way of being and relating.

If not yet, why not now?

Our process is simple. We will take turns reading one paragraph at a time. If reading in public is not your thing, just say "pass, please." We will spend one full minute of silence after each meditation.

Leader: **Triumphant in Death**

Reader:

The passion combat is over and the dragon lion thinks a victory is won. Divinity power shines as the killed Lamb descends into hell itself, breaking down the gates, binding the serpent, and tearing the prey out of enslavement. The true Samson, in death, lays prostrate an army of the enemy. The long awaited bright light shines into every shadow.

reminder: one full minute of silence after each meditation

Rising in Blessedness

The third day dawns on the Lord's sacred sleep of the tomb. On the day of the week both the first and the eighth, lying prostrate the author of life conquers death and opens the door to eternity. A great earthquake and comes an angel of the Lord, attractive and giving comfort to the women and a severe terror to the soldiers. The Lord himself appears to the devoted women, is seen by Peter, then by the disciples on Emmaus Road, then by all the apostles except one, later touched by Thomas proclaiming *My Lord and my God!* For the forty days he shows himself to his disciples and in many ways, eating and drinking with them.

Extraordinary Beauty

The beautiful flower from the root of Jesse has blossomed in the incarnation and withered in the passion, and now blossoms again in the resurrection: the beauty of all. That body subtle and agile is clothed in glory more radiant than the sun, an example of the beauty destined for risen human bodies.

If the just will shine forth like the sun,
how great do you think is the eternal beatitude
of the very Sun of justice himself?
There is no comparison worthy!
Happy indeed the eyes that have seen!

Dominion over the Earth

The Lord appears also in Galilee declaring to
his disciples that all power in heaven and on
earth has been given to him, and sends them
into the whole world to preach the gospel to
every creature, the salvation promise to
believers. In the power of the name of Jesus
Christ is command over all creatures and
diseases. It is to be shown and known all over
the world that the Son of God Jesus Christ lives
and reigns in every place.

Everyone enslaved in any way,
know and tell of your new Joseph!
Everyone wandering over desert sand,
know and tell of your new Moses!
Everyone imprisoned by fear of death,
know and tell of your new David!
And bend your knee
with all on earth and under the earth.

Leader of his Army

Forty days and forty nights beyond our Lord's own resurrection, after appearances in mystic days and again eating with his disciples, the kind Master climbs the Mount of Olives and in their sight lifts up his hands being borne into heaven, a cloud engulfing, and he hides himself from the view of humanity, leading captivity into captivity. The gates are open! The way into the kingdom is made for followers and exiles to be common citizens with angels and saints and members of God's household. The fall of the angels is repaired. The honor of the Father is now eternal. The triumph of our Master is proven: He is the Lord of Hosts.

Lifted Up to Heaven

Angels sing and saints rejoice: the God and Lord of angels and humanity soars on the wings of the wind ascending to the heaven of heavens. Marvelous agile power sits at the right hand of the Father to intercede for us. It is fitting that we should have such a High Priest: holy, innocent, undefiled, and at the right hand of Majesty Itself showing to the glorious face of his Father the scars of wounds suffered for you and for me.

Let every tongue give thanks to you, Father,
for your indescribable gift of charity abundant
sparing not your one begotten Son
but handing him over to death for us all
that we might have before your face in heaven
so great and so faithful an advocate.

Giver of the Spirit

Seven weeks full passing since the resurrection, now on the fiftieth day, the disciples are in one place gathered with Mary the mother of Jesus. Coming to these hundred and twenty men and women is a sound from heaven as of a wind blowing violence. The Spirit descent appears in the form of tongues of fire giving speech to mouth, light to intellect, and ardor to affection. Filled with the Holy Spirit they begin to speak in different languages. The prompting of this Holy Spirit teaches them all truth, inflames them with all love, and strengthens them in every virtue. Aided by this grace, illumination, and power, though few and simple they go forth and plant the Church into the world seedbed by their own blood with words catching fire, the example of truth, and even astonishing miracles. Exceeding beauty and adorned in wonder variety, the Church becomes lovable to her Spouse, and to the enemy awe-full.

Freeing from Guilt

This holy Church, a variety diversified by the Holy Spirit wonder, is yet united in a single whole with one supreme Hierarch presiding: Christ the High Priest. Offices are appointed and Charismatic Gifts are distributed, some as apostles, some as prophets, others again as evangelists, others as pastors and teachers to build up saints and the body of Christ. As the grace of the Holy Spirit is sevenfold, he gives the sacraments as seven remedies to sickness. Through ministry of sacraments he gives sanctifying grace and forgives sins. And since sins are cleansed in the heat of tribulation, as Christ freely exposed himself to suffering waves, so God permits his body, the Church, to suffer tribulation being tested and purified to the end of the world.

So as the patriarchs, the prophets, the apostles,
the martyrs, confessors and virgins,
and as many as have been pleasing to God
have passed through many tribulations
and remained faithful,
so are called all chosen members of Christ
to the day of the Lord.

Pondering Week Five

The Novelty of his Resurrection & The Sublimity of his Ascension

Ponder in silence whether in these meditations something like one of these surfaced:

a seed planted,
> something I anticipate taking root and growing within me, and growing me…

a memory provoked,
> part of my story or our journey, whether pleasant or sad…

a question raised,
> something unknown to study, research, discuss with others, or further ponder…

an action prompted
> or way to consider letting God form me into the person God created me to be…

Allow another three minutes for silent pondering, and then the group may either discuss the ponderings (restraining the urge to "fix" anybody) or stay in silence until time is up.

When time is up: Are there any intercessions from the group?

Our Father … *and a stanza from the song on page 58?*

Lord, when at your Last Sup-per you did pray
That all your Church might be for-ev-er one.
Grant us at ev'-ry Eu-cha-rist to say
With long-ing heart and soul, "your will be done."
O may we all one bread, one bod-y be,
Through this blest Sac-ra-ment of U-ni-ty.

For all your Church, O Lord, we in-ter-cede;
Make all our sad div-is-ions soon to cease;
Draw us the near-er each, to each we plead,
By draw-ing all to you, O Prince of Peace;
Thus may we all one bread, one bod-y be,
Through this blest Sac-ra-ment of U-ni-ty.

We pray for all who wan-der from your fold;
O bring them home,
                    Good Shep-herd of the sheep,
Back to the faith which saints be-lieved of old,
Back to the Church which still the faith does keep;
Soon may we all one bread, one bod-y be,
Through this blest Sac-ra-ment of U-ni-ty.

So, Lord, at length when sac-ra-ments shall cease,
May we be one with all your Church a-bove,
One with your saints in one un-bro-ken peace,
One with your saints in one un-bound-ed love;
More bless-ed still in peace and love to be
One with the Trin-i-ty in U-ni-ty.

Text: William H. Turton, 1859-1938, altered
Music: 10 10 10 10 10 10 UNDE ET MEMORES, William H. Monk, 1823-1899

WEEK SIX

11th Fruit: The Equity of his Judgment
Truthful Witness, Wrathful Judge,
Glorious Conqueror, Adorned Spouse
12th Fruit: The Eternity of his Kingdom
King and Son of the King, Inscribed Book,
Fountain-Ray of Light, Desired End

Opening Meditation from page 7.

Song from page 74.

Leader: God has a plan.
Each of us is a part of that plan.

Just in case no one has ever
said this to you, God loves you.

Sooner or later, each of us will be called
in the shared priesthood of the baptized
to forgive, always by God's grace.

If not yet, why not now?

Our process is simple. We will take turns
reading one paragraph at a time. If reading in
public is not your thing, just say "pass, please."
We will spend one full minute of silence after
each meditation.

Leader: **Truthful Witness**

Reader:

When time for the future judgment, fire
preceding judge, angels sent with trumpets,
and elect gathered from the four winds, God
will judge the secrets of hearts. All in their
tombs will rise by the power of the divine
command and stand before the judgment seat.

Things hidden in shadows will be illumined;
the counsels of hearts will be revealed;
books of consciences will be opened
with that book called the book of life.
In an instant
all the secrets of all will be revealed to all
with such clear certainty that against
truth testimony of Christ and conscience
not a single path will be open
for denial, defense, excuse, or subterfuge;
each will receive according to his or her deeds.
There is imposed on us, then,
the great necessity to be good,
since all our actions are in view
of the all-seeing Judge.

reminder: one full minute of silence after each meditation

Wrathful Judge

When the sign of the omnipotent Son of God does appear in the clouds, heavens are shaken, earth engulfs in conflagration, and comes a division of all the just on one side and the wicked on the other, then the Judge of the universe will appear as wrath to the reprobate and justice to those of good virtue.

The Judge will appear,
the one Judge righteous to be wrathful;
hell to open in chaos and heaven in beauty;
sins will accuse and goodness will testify;
where will the sinner flee?
Is there any real wondering to fear but this one:
Is it ever too late to flee to God's mercy?

Glorious Conqueror

Is the condemnation of enemies of God to eternal flames everlasting the promised penalty? Will the just bathe their hands in the blood of sinners? Will the victorious Lamb make his enemies his footstool? Is this glory?

[A teacher wise in the ways of God says:
"We believe there is a hell
and we pray that no one is there."
Mercy is the ultimate power, ultimate glory.]
You on your living journey,
will you fall prey to seductive deceit
or say your own fidelity "yes" to the truth
of the infinite mercy of God?

Adorned Spouse

When finally the face of the earth is renewed,
when light of the moon is like light of the sun
and the light of the one sun is like that of seven
and that holy city Jerusalem from heaven
is made ready for the marriage of the Lamb,
adorned as a bride in the double stole
of beatific vision and body glorified,
she will be led into the palace,
into the sacred bridal chamber
for a union so intense a covenant
that bride and groom will become one spirit.
Christ is clothed
in multi-color beauty of the elect
and the sweet wedding song will sing
Alleluia!

King and Son of the King

See the noble eternal glory of God's kingdom
in the dignity of its King. On his garment and
on his thigh are written King of kings and Lord
of lords, power everlasting, whom all tribes
and peoples and tongues will serve always, a
King of peace on whose face all long to gaze.

How glorious is the kingdom
where all the just reign
with this King beyond excellence by law
of truth, peace, charity, life, and eternity,
undivided by those who reign,
unlessened by being shared,
undisturbed by multitude variety,
not disordered by inequity of rank,
uncircumscribed by space,
unchanged by motion,
and unmeasured by time.

Inscribed Book

The kingdom is governed by the brilliant rays of law perfected by the light of wisdom written in Christ Jesus as in the book of life, in which God the Father has deposited all the treasures of wisdom and knowledge. The only-begotten Son of God, the uncreated Word, is the book of wisdom and light full of the principles alive in the mind of the supreme Crafter. The manifold wisdom of God shines forth from him and in him.

If only I could find this book of eternal origin,
incorruptible essence, living knowledge,
indelible script, easy teaching, sweet knowing,
inscrutable depth, ineffable words,
yet all a single Word!
Truly, whoever finds this book will find life
and will draw salvation from the Lord.

Fountain-Ray of Light

All good and perfect gifts come from the Father of Lights in abundant plenty through Jesus Christ the superessential Ray who is one, can do all things, and renews all things while himself perduring.

You soul devoted to God,
run with living desire to this Font of light
and cry from the center of your heart,
"O inaccessible beauty of the most high God
and pure brightness of eternal light,
life keeping alive all life,
light enlightening every light
and lighting from before the dawn of light
thousands of thousands shining lights
before the throne of your Godness!
You of bottomless depth, limitless height,
unboundable breadth and unstainable purity,
your heavenly banquet guests
drink to joyful inebriation
and sing to unceasing jubilation.
Anoint us with this sacred oil;
refresh our thirsty-throated hearts
that we may sing a canticle of praise:

With you is the fountain of life,
and in your light we will see light."

Desired End

The end of all desires is happiness, "a perfect state with the presence of all goods," reached only by ultimate union with the Alpha and the Omega, the origin of goods of nature and grace, body and spirit, in time and in eternity. He is truthfully called Jesus.

Beloved Jesus,
believing and hoping and loving
with mind and heart and strength and soul,
may I be carried to you
who alone are goal-sufficient and good
to those who seek you and love your name.

You, my good Jesus,
redeem the lost,
save the redeemed,
give hope to exiles
and strength to laborers
and solace to anguished spirits;
you crown the triumphant in dignity
and reward the citizens of heaven with joy,
you, the offspring of God,
the fruit of the virginal womb,
and the fountain abundant with all graces
of whose fullness we have all received.

Leader: **Prayer to the Holy Spirit**

All: **Father and Son,**
out of your treasure of grace
send your Holy Spirit:

with the gift of **WISDOM**
that we may taste the fruit of the tree of life;

with the gift of **UNDERSTANDING**
for illumination of the intentions of our mind;

with the gift of **COUNSEL**
so we may know the right paths to follow;

with the gift of **FORTITUDE**
to hold peacefully firm when times are tough;

with the gift of **KNOWLEDGE**
that we may learn to discern good from evil;

with the gift of **PIETY**
so that our hearts may grow full of mercy;

with the gift of **FEAR OF THE LORD**
that is our peace.

To you, Lord Jesus,
God incarnate, crucified, and glorified,
with the Father and the Holy Spirit,
be honor and glory,
thanksgiving, beauty and power,
forever and ever. Amen.

Pondering Week Six

The Equity of his Judgment & The Eternity of his Kingdom

Ponder in silence whether in these meditations
something like one of these surfaced:

a seed planted,
> something I anticipate taking root and
> growing within me, and growing me...

a memory provoked,
> part of my story or our journey,
> whether pleasant or sad...

a question raised,
> something unknown
> to study, research, discuss with others,
> or further ponder...

an action prompted
> or resolution made, a way to claim
> my identity as a daughter/son of God...

*Allow another three minutes for silent pondering,
and then the group may either discuss the ponderings
(restraining the urge to "fix" anybody)
or stay in silence until time is up.*

When time is up: Are there any intercessions
                      from the group?

Our Father ... *and a stanza from the song on page 74?*

Sources

Bonaventure, *The Soul's Journey Into God, The Tree of Life, The Life of St. Francis,* translation and introduction by Ewert Cousins, preface by Ignatius Brady, O.F.M., part of the 60 volume *The Classics of Western Spirituality: A Library of the Great Spiritual Masters,* New York: Paulist Press, 1978, 353 pages.

Ewert Cousins is one of the many excellent seminary teachers from my five years at Mundelein Seminary north of Chicago. His teaching has proven an inspiration in spiritual direction and in preaching. According to Dr. Cousins,

> Bonaventure's Latin…is highly complex, composed of long stately sentences, with rhythmically balanced phrases and clusters of symbols whose meaning is enhanced by the subtle relations suggested by their position in the rhetorical structure. *pg. 47*

He shot for a more literal translation, but using sense lines to help the reader meditate. Though I honestly love it, it also has the kind of weight medieval works tend to have. One hope for this paraphrase is that it can serve as a first-read introduction that will send readers to Dr. Ewert Cousins' real translation. Ewert went to glory in 2009.

Who is Saint Bonaventure?

Born around 1218 at Bagnorea in Tuscany, Bonaventure (the name means "good luck") studied in Paris and taught his fellow members of the Order of Friars Minor. While the Franciscans Minister General he continued to be a prolific writer. *The Soul's Journey into God* is generally considered his masterpiece. An advisor to King St. Louis, he begged his way out of being Archbishop of York, but was serving as Cardinal-Archbishop of Albano when he died at the Council of Lyons in 1274. His memorial is celebrated on July 14.

Opening Meditation

Pg 7, *Imagine a tree…,* from paragraph #3 of Cousins *The Tree of Life,*
See Revelation 22:1-2, Esther 10:6, Genesis 2:9-10

Mystery of the Incarnation

Pg. 13, *Sent from Heaven,* see Matthew 1:18-23 and Luke 1:26-38
      fullness of time - Galatians 4:4
      power of the Most High - Luke 1:35
      my soul is stretched… - Luke 1:46

Pg. 15, *Born of Mary,* see Luke 2:1-18
      quiet silence - Wisdom 18:14
      like a bridegroom - Psalm 19:6
      Glory to God in the highest… - Luke 2:14

Pg. 16, *Conformed to his Ancestors*
      circumcised - Luke 2:21
      what, dust and ash… - Sirach 10:9

Pg. 17, *Shown to the Magi,* see Matthew 2:1-12

Pg. 18, *Submissive to the Law,* see Luke 2:27, Gal. 4:5, Romans 8:21
      now dismiss your servant… - Luke 2:29

Pg. 19, *Exiled from his Kingdom,* see Matthew 2:13-23
      causes sorrow… - Luke 2:48

Pg. 24, *Heavenly Baptist,* see Matt. 3:13-17, Mark 1:9-11, Luke 3:21-22
      confer…regenerative power - Bede, *In Lucem,* I, 3:21
      and hear…up to you - Pseudo-Anselm, *Meditationes,* 15

Pg. 25, *Tempted by the Enemy,* see Matt. 4:1-11, Mk 1:12-13, Lk 4:1-13
      tested as we are… - Hebrews 4:15

Pg. 26, *Wonderful in his Miracles*
      things of marvel - Psalm 71:18
      Lord, if you wish… - Luke 5:12, Matthew 8:2
      Lord, my servant boy… - Matthew 8:6
      Son of David, have mercy on me. - Matthew 15:22
      If I touch his garment… - Matthew 9:21
      See, Lord, the one you love is ill. - John 11:3

Pg. 27, *Transfigured,* see Matthew 17:1-8, Mark 9:1-13, Luke 9:28-36
      Lord, it is good for us to be here. - Matthew 17:4

Mystery of the Incarnation, continued

Pg. 29, *The Solicitous Shepherd,* see Luke 15:4-10, Mt 18:12-14, John 10
        The good shepherd gives his life... - John 10:11
        Like a shepherd he will feed his flock. - Isaiah 40:11
        call of Matthew - Matthew 9:9-13
        Zaccheus - Luke 19:1-10
        the sinful woman at his feet - John 8:3-11
        Nor do I condemn you... - John 8:10-11

Pg. 30, *Bathed with Tears,* see John 11:35, Luke 19:41, Hebrews 5:7

Pg. 31, *Acclaimed King of the World,* see Matthew 21:1-11,
                        Mark 11:1-11, Luke 19:29-38, John 12:12-16

Pg. 32, *Consecrated Bread,* see Matthew 26:17-29, Mark 14:12-25,
                                Luke 22:7-38, John 13-17
        As a deer longs for springs of water... - Psalm 42:2

Mystery of his Passion

Pg. 36, *Sold through Guile,* see Mt 26:14-16, Mk 14:10-11, Lk 22:3-6

Pg. 37, *Prostrate in Prayer,* see Matthew 26:36-46, Mark 14:32-42,
                                Luke 22:40-46, John 18:1-4
        hallel psalms - Mark 14:26, Psalms 114-118
        ...Father if it is possible - Matthew 26:39, Luke 22:42
        ...carried our sorrows... - Isaiah 53:4

Pg. 39, *Surrounded by the Mob,* see Matthew 26:47-56, Mark 14:43-52,
                                Luke 22:47-53, John 18:2-11
        men of blood - Psalm 55:24

Pg. 40, *Bound with Chains*
        Judas is so bitter... - Matthew 27:3-5

Pg. 41, *Denied by his Own,* see Matthew 26:69-75, Mark 14:66-72,
                                Luke 22:56-62, John 18:12-27
        bitter...inebriation - Lamentation 3:15

Pg. 42, *Blindfolded,* see Matthew 26:57-68, Mark 14:53-65,
                                Luke 22:66-71, John 18:13,19-24

Pg. 43, *Handed Over to Pilate,* see Matthew 27:11-26, Mark 15:1-15,
                                             Luke 23:1-5, John 18:28-19:16
          …We have no king but Caesar! - John 19:15
          …Away with him! Crucify him! - John 19:15

Pg. 44, *Condemned to Death,* see Luke 23:8-25, Matthew 27:26-31,
                                             Mark 15:16-20, John 19:1-16
          …what he did not steal. - Psalm 69:5

Pg. 48, *Scorned by All,* see John 19:15

Pg. 49, *Nailed to the Cross,* see Matthew 27:33-37, Mark 15:22-26,
                                             Luke 23:33-34, John 19:17-24
          be my longing – Job 6:8

Pg. 50, *Linked with Thieves,* see Mt 27:38-44, Mk 15:27-32, Lk 23:34-43

Pg. 51, *Given Gall to Drink,* see Matt 27:48, Mark 15:36, John 19:28-30
          I thirst. - John 19:28
          It is consummated. - John 19:30
          Woman, behold your son. - John 19:26

Pg. 52, *Sun Dimmed in Death,* see Matthew 27:50-53, Mark 15:37-39,
                                             Luke 23:44-47, John 19:30
          your Anointed - Palm 84:10

Pg. 53, *Pierced with a Lance,* see John 19:31-37
          the fountain of living water springing up
                    to eternal life - John 4:14
          be like the dove… - Jeremiah 48:28
          the sparrow finding a home - Psalm 84:4
          draw the saving water - Isaiah 12:3
          this river - Genesis 2:10

Pg. 55, *Dressed in Blood*
          robe red like that of a wine presser - Isaiah 63:2
          beast-bloody tunic of Joseph - Genesis 37:31

Pg. 56, *Laid in the Tomb,* see Matthew 27:57-66, 28:1, Mark 15:42-47,
                                             Luke 23:50-56, 24:1, John 19:38-20:1

Mystery of his Glory

Pg. 60, *Triumphant in Death*
>> the true Samson... - Judges 16:30
>> the bright light shines - Isaiah 9:1

Pg. 61, *Rising in Blessedness,* see Matthew 28:1-20, Mark 16:1-18,
>> Luke 24:1-49, John 20:1-31, 21:1-25
>> My Lord and my God! - John 20:28

Pg. 63, *Extraordinary Beauty*
>> flower of the root of Jesse - Isaiah 11:1
>> the just will shine forth like the sun - Matthew 13:43
>> glory more radiant than the sun - see Wisdom 7:29

Pg. 65, *Dominion over the Earth*
>> The Lord appears also in Galilee... - Matthew 28:16-20
>> sending them...to every creature - Mark 16:15
>> command over all creatures and diseases - Mark 16:20
>> in every place - Psalm 103:22
>> bend your knee with all - see Philippians 2:10

Pg. 66, *Leader of his Army,* see Acts 1:9-11
>> lifts up his hands being borne into heaven - Luke 24:50-51
>> captivity into captivity - Psalm 68:19
>> and members of God's household - Ephesians 2:19

Pg. 67, *Lifted Up to Heaven*
>> to the heaven of heavens - Psalm 68:34
>> to intercede for us - Hebrews 1:4, 9:24
>> It is fitting...such a High Priest... - Hebrews 7:26
>> Let every tongue give thanks...so faithful an advocate.
>> - see Pseudo-Anselm, *Medi.,* 9, Romans 8:32, 1 John 2:1

Pg. 69, *Giver of the Spirit*
>> a sound from heaven...wind... - Acts 1:14, 2:2
>> hundred and twenty... - Acts 1:15
>> filled with the Holy Spirit...different languages - Acts 2:4
>> by their own blood - *Brev. Rom.,* Apostles, noc. 3, resp. 1
>> wonder variety - Psalm 45:15
>> and to the enemy awe-full - see Song of Songs 6:10

Sources

Pg. 71, *Freeing from Guilt*
>Offices…Charismatic Gifts… - see Ephesians 4:11-12

Pg. 77, *Truthful Witness*
>fire will precede…from the four winds
>>- Psalm 97:3, Matthew 24:31, Mark 13:27
>
>things hidden will be revealed - 1 Corinthians 4:5
>the book of life - Revelation 20:12
>according to his or her deeds
>>- Psalm 62:13, Romans 2:6, Revelation 2:23
>
>There is imposed on us…of the all-seeing Judge.
>>- Boethius, *De consolation philosophiae*, V, prosa 6.

Pg. 78, *Wrathful Judge,* see Matt. 24:29-31, Mark 13:24-27, Lk 21:25-28
>heavens are shaken - Matthew 24:29
>The Judge will…where will the sinner flee?
>>- based on authentic Anselm, *Meditationes*, 1, and Pseudo-Bernard, *Tractatus de interior domo*, c 22, no. 46, 1 Peter 4:18

Pg. 79, *Glorious Conqueror,* see Matthew 13:24-30, 36-43
>Will the just bathe their hands… - see Psalm 58:11
>enemies his footstool? - Psalm 110:1

Pg. 80, *Adorned Spouse*
>light of the moon…marriage of the Lamb
>>- Isaiah 30:26, Revelation 21:10, 19:7
>
>double stole - Bonaventure, *Breviloquium*, VII, 7, no. 1
>multi-colored - Genesis 37:3, and see Ezekiel 16:13

Pg. 81, *King, Son of the King*
>King of kings and Lord of lords - Revelation 19:16
>power everlasting - Daniel 7:14
>all tribes and peoples and tongues - Revelation 7:9
>on whose face all long to gaze - 1 Kings 10:24

Pg. 83, *Inscribed Book*
>all the treasures of wisdom and knowledge - Colossians 2:3
>manifold wisdom of God - Ephesians 3:10
>find life…draw salvation from the Lord - Proverbs 8:35

Mystery of his Glory, continued

Pg. 85, *Fountain-Ray of Light*

All good...from the Father of Lights - James 1:17
one, can do...while himself perduring - Wisdom 7:27
O inaccessible beauty...and unstainable purity
 - Pseudo-Anselm, *Meditationes, 9*
With you...we will see light - Psalm 36:10

Pg. 86, *Desired End*

a perfect state with the presence of all good
 - Boethius, *De con.,* III, prosa 2.
Alpha and Omega - Revelation 1:8
mind...heart...strength...soul -Mt 22:37, Mk 12:30, Lk 10:27
love your name - Psalm 5:12
of whose fullness we have all received
 - Pseudo-Anselm, *Meditationes,* 9, John 1:16

Pg. 89, *Prayer to the Holy Spirit,* see Isaiah 11:2

Stephen Joseph Wolf is a parish priest, spiritual director and retreat leader in the Diocese of Nashville, where he grew up the second of eight sons of a parish secretary and Nashville's best television repairman, and has worked as a paper boy, janitor, laundry worker, desk clerk, landscaper, accountant and priest. He writes for faith sharing groups and retreats and spiritual direction on weekly "monk days" of silence and solitude.

Prayer Books:

A Simple Family Breviary*
A Jesus Breviary
Hinge Hours for Ordinary Time
Hinge Hour Singer*
Psalter of Lectio, Revised*
Best of the Psalter*
Gospel of Life Prayer Cycle

*pdf Samples of these are available at **www.idjc.org**.

Faith-Sharing Books (*arranged for six weeks*):

1. **Tree of Life**
   Incarnation, Passion & Glory
   Saint Bonaventure on the Christ Story

2. **Pondering Our Faith, Revised with the New Creed**
   The New Evangelization
   The Church
   Sacraments
   Vocation
   Moral Formation in Christ
   The Sacred

3. **Forty Penances for Spiritual Exercise**
   God's Complete Love: A Reality
   Reality of Sin and Reconciliation
   Universal Call to Holiness
   Vocation "Yes"
   Perfect Act of Love
   Whole New Way

4. **God's Money: where faith meets life in the world**
   Micah's Vine & Fig Tree
   Daily Bread This Day
   Building a Bigger Barn
   Parables of Stewards
   When Life is Changed
   Community of Believers

5. **Being Spouses: from celibate observation**
   Marriage Sacramentality
   The Domestic Church
   Permanence
   Fidelity
   Children
   Intimacy

6. **Twelve-Step Spirituality for Christians**
   When I Am Weak
   Let Go and Let God
   Sick As Our Secrets
   Progress, Not Perfection
   Let It Begin With Me
   One Day at a Time

7. **Anger-Grief the Jesus Way** (*based on Mark 3:1-6*)
   A Sabbath Assembly
   Being Watched
   Invited by Jesus
   Riddle Silence
   Anger-Grief
   Turning to Freedom

8. **Planning My Own Funeral?** (*Four Weeks*)
   Vigil   Readings   Eucharist   Left Behind

9. **God's Ones: a *So-What* Book for the Baptized**
   Coming soon.